BRITISH LIBRARY MONOGRAPH NO. 1

DAVID GARRICK
1717-1779
A brief account

by
HELEN R. SMITH

The British Library

Cover illustration

Front: *Garrick as Bayes in Buckingham's 'The Rehearsal'* *Drawing by J. Roberts* (British Museum, Dept. of Prints and Drawings)

Back: *Garrick as Sir John Brute in Vanbrugh's 'The Provok'd Wife'* *Drawing by J. Roberts* (British Museum, Dept. of Prints and Drawings)

© 1979 The British Library Board
ISBN 0 904654 40 0
Published by the British Library
Reference Division Publications, Great Russell Street
London WC1B 3DG

British Library Cataloguing in Publication Data
Smith, Helen R.
David Garrick, 1717-1779
1. Garrick, David
2. Actors – England – Biography
3. Authors, English – 18th century – Biography
I. Title   II. British Library. *Reference Division*
792'.028' 0924   PN 2598.G3

Designed by Frank Phillips
Set in 11/12pt Monotype Garamond
Printed in Great Britain at
The Stellar Press Ltd, Hatfield

Contents

60

Foreword

This brief account was written to accompany the British Library's exhibition held in the King's Library from 30th November 1979 – 11th May 1980 to commemorate the bicentenary of the death of David Garrick. The exhibition celebrates Garrick's bequest to the British Museum in 1779 of his statue of Shakespeare by Roubiliac, and of his fine collection of early English plays.

Unless otherwise acknowledged the illustrations are of items in the British Library's collections, and were photographed by its Photographic Service.

The British Library Board wishes to thank the following for their generosity in lending objects for the exhibition or providing photographs:

The Ashmolean Museum, Oxford
The Trustees of the British Museum
The Fitzwilliam Museum, Cambridge
The Viscount Lambton
The Museum of London
The National Portrait Gallery
The Public Record Office
The Victoria and Albert Museum
Mrs Michael Wynne

The quotation from *Lichtenberg's Visits to England as described in his Letters and Diaries*, translated by Margaret L. Mare and W. H. Quarrell, 1938, is included by permission of Oxford University Press.

The author would like to acknowledge with gratitude the assistance received in writing this account from Dorothy Anderson, John Barr and Hugh Tait.

1 Engraved roundel of Garrick admiring Shakespeare, possibly designed as a watch-paper (British Museum. Dept. of Prints and Drawings)

Introduction

David Garrick, the most celebrated actor-manager England has ever produced, rose from relatively humble beginnings to a pre-eminent position in the social and artistic life of eighteenth-century London. When he died in 1779, his funeral procession stretched from the Adelphi in the Strand to Westminster Abbey; and a duke and three earls were among the pall-bearers. Garrick was buried in the Abbey at the foot of Scheemakers' memorial to William Shakespeare. As Sheridan wrote in *Verses to the Memory of Garrick*:

> . . . Shakespear's image from its hallow'd base,
> Seem'd to prescribe the grave, and point the place.

Throughout his career Garrick's reputation had grown with that of his idol, Shakespeare [2], largely because of his brilliant performances in Shakespearian roles. When by the end of the century the plays of Shakespeare had been firmly established in the English theatrical repertoire, and a start had been made towards restoring full and accurate performing texts, much of the credit was due to Garrick.

2 Garrick as Steward of the Stratford Jubilee 1769. Mezzotint by J. Saunders after Benjamin Van der Gucht 1773

7

Garrick's Appearance and Character

What was Garrick like? He was short, probably not more than five feet four inches in height, and well proportioned, although he became rather stocky in later life. His acting ability almost completely disguised his shortness. It is agreed that his most remarkable features were his bright and piercing dark eyes and his mobile and expressive face. Like most actors he shaved his head, except for a lock at the back to anchor the wigs he wore both in performance and in private life. Despite his wealth, his dress was always unostentatious. The elegant plain brown velvet suit he was wearing when painted by Pompeo Batoni in Rome in 1764 is preserved in the Museum of London. The portrait is now in the Ashmolean Museum. He lived in a style which befitted his large income, but without undue extravagance.

Garrick was charming and lively; witty, but not of outstanding intellectual power, yet a most entertaining conversationalist. He had an overwhelming desire to please and to be liked; his corresponding dread of criticism made him go to inordinate lengths to be conciliating and also made him susceptible to flattery. When conducting his business affairs, in order to give himself time to think, he cultivated an abrupt broken delivery, which provoked many amusing accounts and parodies.

In private life he loved to play jokes on his friends and indulge his talent for mimicry. Fanny Burney describes how well he took off Samuel Johnson in the act of borrowing and maltreating his precious books: 'uttering a Latin ejaculation . . . in a fit of enthusiasm, – over his head

GARRICK.   SHAKESPEAR.

goes poor Petrarca, – Russia leather and all!' There is perhaps a trace of bitterness in another Johnson imitation heard both by Boswell and Charlotte Burney: 'Davy has some convivial pleasantries in him; but 'tis a futile fellow'. He wished very much to be taken seriously in Johnson's circle.

That Garrick was a gentleman born undoubtedly helped him in his social advancement, by which he set great store. He did not, however, boast of his successes. As his family was without wealth or influence, these were due entirely to the exercise of his natural abilities.

3 Garrick without his wig after Johann Zoffany, facing Shakespeare. Engraving by J. S. Müller

Garrick's Early Career

David Garrick was born on 19th February 1717 at the Angel Inn [4] at Hereford, the third child and second son of Peter and Arabella Garrick. His father, an army officer, was on a recruiting expedition, and he and his wife were away from their home in her native Lichfield. The Garrick family were recent immigrants of Huguenot origin, and Arabella Clough was the daughter of a canon of Lichfield Cathedral. Apart from the year 1725, spent with an uncle who was a merchant in Lisbon, it was at Lichfield that David spent a happy childhood in a large, poor, but affectionate family. From the age of sixteen he was virtually the head of the family, since his father went to serve in Gibraltar and his elder brother Peter was in the Navy. Whilst still at Lichfield Grammar School, David assumed a responsibility for the younger members, which, in the case of his brother George, he was never to lose. In 1735 Captain Garrick returned home in poor health and sent David and George as pupils to the small school at Edial recently opened by their old family friend Samuel Johnson. Garrick was certainly no scholar, and Johnson was not temperamentally suited to teaching a group of lively boys. Thus in 1737 Garrick, who had recently inherited £1,000 from his uncle, and Johnson, who was only nine years his senior, set out together for London to seek their fortunes. They had with them barely more than the money for the journey and on arrival in London had to borrow five pounds from a bookseller. Garrick was to go on to Rochester to be coached by John Colson, the headmaster of the grammar school, pre-

GARRICK'S BIRTH PLACE,
HEREFORD.

paratory to studying law.

Soon, however, his master was offered a Chair at Cambridge. Garrick's studies ended and he returned to London. Although he had entered his name at Lincoln's Inn, he abandoned the law and used his legacy to found a wine business in Durham Yard (later pulled down to make way for the Adelphi), in partnership with his brother Peter, who had just inherited £1,000 from their father. It was probably through soliciting business in the many taverns and coffee houses in nearby Covent Garden that Garrick met and began to make friends with the staff of the two major theatres. His biographers tell of his performance as Sergeant Kite in a children's production of Farquhar's *The Recruiting Officer* in Lichfield at the age of eleven, and it is obvious that he was drawn naturally towards the theatrical world. He was encouraged by Johnson's employer, Edward Cave, the founder of *The Gentleman's Magazine,* to act and to write prologues and

4 *The Angel Inn at Hereford: Garrick's birthplace. Engraving by J. Storer 1823*

11

even plays, and this probably helped him break into the acting community. He soon came to know the actor Charles Macklin, who offered advice and friendship; and he cultivated the managers of the playhouses. Clearly his ambition was to act, and at first secretly, in the face of strong family opposition, he began to work towards realizing it.

On 19th October 1741 the announcement that Richard III at Goodman's Fields Theatre in Ayliffe Street in Whitechapel would be played by 'a gentleman (who never appear'd on any stage)' was not strictly true. Garrick afterwards recounted how he had during the previous season performed the masked pantomime role of Harlequin as a substitute for Richard Yates. During the summer of 1741, under the name of Lydall, the maiden name of his manager's wife, he had gained experience in playing at least nine parts with Henry Giffard's company at Ipswich. From this brief preparation Garrick's vigorous and exciting King Richard [5] emerged to astound London. He drew the fashionable audiences away from the officially licensed theatres in Drury Lane and Covent Garden to attend 'free' performances, sandwiched in the middle of the concerts for which admission was charged. The effect of his new naturalness and vivacity on audiences accustomed to solemn declamation and gesture was remarkable. Alexander Pope said of Garrick's performance: 'That young man never had his equal, and he never will have a rival'. London was conquered. James Quin [7], a great and stately actor of the old school, was forced to admit: 'If the fellow is right, I and the rest of the players have been all wrong'. Although he and Garrick acted together for the 1746–47 season, and, in parts like Falstaff, Quin was supreme, by 1751 he had conceded defeat and retired to Bath leaving Garrick's position unassailable. The two men became good friends once their stage rivalry was over and it was Garrick who wrote Quin's epitaph.

Garrick was not the first to experiment with a more natural style of acting. Earlier, on 14th February 1741, Macklin had surprised audiences with a villainous rather than a comic Shylock [6]. With less talent and grace than

5 *Garrick as Richard III. Engraving by William Hogarth and C. Grignion after Hogarth*

6 *Charles Macklin as Shylock. Engraving after Johann Ludwig Fäsch*

7 *James Quin.
Mezzotint by
J. Faber after
Thomas Hudson*

Garrick, Macklin was never able to sustain his popularity with audiences and his quarrelsome temperament continually led to troubles with the managers. The young Garrick owed a great deal to Macklin's advice and coaching. His first tentative performances as King Lear in 1742 were speedily corrected by the more experienced actor, until the part became his greatest triumph. His friendship with Macklin was not, however, to last.

When the jealous managers of the licensed theatres had Goodman's Fields closed down at the end of Garrick's first season, he signed a contract to perform at Drury

Lane. By this time he had become associated with the attractive, generous but promiscuous Margaret (Peg) Woffington [8], an Irish-born actress in that company, and they spent a successful summer season together at the Smock Alley Theatre in Dublin. On their return to England they set up house in Bow Street. For part of the season Macklin lived in the same house; the three held similar views about reforming acting standards, and they may have shared housekeeping expenses, but it is wrong to assume that they formed a *ménage à trois*.

8 Peg Woffington. Mezzotint by J. Faber after J. G. Eccard. Her book is tooled with a representation of a statue of Shakespeare

9 *Charles Macklin
aged 92.
Engraving
by J. Condé after
John Opie*

10 *Eva Maria
Garrick.
Engraving by
W. P. Sherlock
after Catherine
Read*

When Charles Fleetwood, the manager at **Drury Lane**, found himself unable to pay the salaries, Garrick and Macklin were involved in the resulting complicated dispute. The actors went on strike, and, although when a settlement was reached most of them were re-employed, the troublesome Macklin was made scapegoat. He bitterly accused Garrick of going back on the strike agreement, and a public quarrel was eventually settled in Garrick's favour by hired mobs in the pit. The relationship between the two men remained uncomfortable for the rest of their lives. Macklin acted and had his plays produced under Garrick as manager, but lost no oppor-

Mrs Garrick.

From the Original Picture by Cath.^e Reid,
in the possession of J. Edwards Esqr

tunity to laugh at or attack him and was the source of many malicious and untrue anecdotes. Macklin gave up the stage for tavern-keeping between 1753 and 1758, but bankruptcy forced him to return. He continued acting until he was at least eighty-nine[9], and was probably a hundred years old when he died.

The affair between Garrick and Peg Woffington did not prosper either. Many writers believe that Garrick originally hoped to marry her. No letters survive, but probably Garrick's prudence and increasing search for respectability came into conflict with her carelessness, and they decided to part in 1745, after three years together. They remained friends, although Garrick would never afterwards speak of their earlier relationship. Peg Woffington continued to act until illness forced her to retire; she died in 1760, aged little more than forty.

During the 1740s Garrick's acting continued to develop in range and power and he was able to save from his substantial salary. He moved between the two London theatres and even spent the winter season of 1745–46 in Dublin in partnership with Thomas Sheridan. On his return, he was able to earn and raise enough money in a season at Covent Garden to accept in 1747 an offer from James Lacy, the new patentee, for a half share in the Drury Lane management. He had by then met and fallen in love with the beautiful and graceful leading dancer at the Haymarket Theatre, 'La Violette' or 'Violetti'. Eva Maria Veigel [10], who returned his affection, was born in Vienna on 29th February 1724. She came to England in 1746, perhaps to escape the attentions of the Emperor Frederick I, and performed with success at the Haymarket and then at Drury Lane. Unexpectedly she was taken up by the eccentric Lady Burlington. Although she continued to dance, she went to live at Burlington House, and it was with the Earl and Countess that Garrick had to negotiate a generous marriage contract, before they would allow their protégée to throw herself away on an actor. It was a long courtship, for the couple were not married until 22nd June 1749.

The marriage was ideally happy, Eva Maria, her gentle charm and self-effacing modesty providing the quiet reassurance and support which Garrick needed, made a perfect foil for his greater ebullience. The couple are credited with never having spent a night apart in nearly thirty years of marriage 'despite temptations'. Their one great unhappiness was their inability to have children. Both loved to have children around them, and visitors to Hampton often described the house or garden as overrun with nephews and nieces – usually the children of the improvident George Garrick, for whose education his brother provided. Henry Angelo, Lætitia Hawkins and, in particular, Fanny Burney, who knew Garrick in their childhood, have left entertaining descriptions of his many kindnesses. Fanny Burney's *Early diary* shows how fond her family was of him, and it was perhaps the strong impression he made on the second Charles Burney in his youth which led to the formation of the latter's large theatrical collection including playbills, engravings, newspaper cuttings and carefully compiled notes of performances, with a volume devoted to each year of Garrick's acting career. This collection, still invaluable to Garrick scholars and theatrical historians, came to the British Museum in 1820 and most of it is now in the British Library.

After their marriage, the Garricks moved into a house at 27 Southampton Street which they ultimately found too small and uncomfortably near the theatre, so that in 1772 they made their London home at 5 (afterwards 4) Adelphi Terrace, in the Adam brothers' grandiose Thamesside project. In 1751 the couple visited Paris on a sightseeing expedition, but they were already thinking of finding a country retreat in England. In 1753 they rented Hampton House [11] on the banks of the Thames in Middlesex and the next year purchased it outright. The house was extensively altered and improved, and they loved to spend their weekends and summers there. The Adam brothers provided a new classical frontage with a pediment and pilasters, and an orangery, and redecorated some of the interior. The gardens were laid out by 'Capability' Brown and a tunnel was made under the main road which unfortunately divided the house from its riverside lawns. Here Garrick constructed his Temple

(Overleaf)
11 Hampton House.
Aquatint by
J. C. Stadler after
J. Farington 1793

J. Farington R.A. delt.   Pub. June 1. 1793. by J. & J. Boydell.   The late Mr G.

...CKS Villa.   *Shakspeare Gallery Pall Mall & Cheapside.*   *J. C. Stadler sculp.*

12 Shakespeare by
Louis François
Roubiliac 1758.
Life size
(British Museum.
Dept. of Medieval
and Later
Antiquities)

13 Roubiliac holding
a model of a
Shakespeare statue
1762.
Painting by
Adrien
Carpentiers
(National
Portrait Gallery)

of Shakespeare, octagonal in shape, with a domed roof and a portico with eight elegant Ionic columns, in which his growing collection of Shakespearian relics was housed.

To preside over the Temple, Garrick commissioned a statue [12] from the Huguenot refugee, Louis François Roubiliac, probably the greatest sculptor working in eighteenth-century England. Roubiliac's best work is to be found in his funeral monuments in Westminster Abbey and elsewhere, and in his informal portrait busts. By 1758, when Garrick's Shakespeare statue was completed, Roubiliac was nearing the end of his career and had financial worries. The statue, which is one of his rare treatments of an imaginary subject, or indeed of a full-length figure, perhaps reveals a certain indecisiveness in its composition. Writers agree that Garrick almost certainly suggested and set the pose showing the poet at the moment of inspiration. Even though Reynolds painted a copy of the Chandos portrait of Shakespeare for the sculptor, and Roubiliac, not satisfied, also executed one himself, the resulting head has something of what a Stratford critic called a 'frenchified' air. The maquette now in the Victoria and Albert Museum was probably the first model for the statue and seems to have a little more vigour.

Garrick paid £315 for the work. As the head was being carved, the marble suddenly revealed a patch of blue veins. 'Ha!' said Garrick, who was continually in and out of the workshop, 'Mulberries!' Some authorities state that Roubiliac offered to replace the head at his own expense.

Adrien Carpentiers painted an interesting portrait of Roubiliac [13], now in the National Portrait Gallery, holding a Shakespeare maquette, but as this is dated 1762 it may show a later reworking of the same subject for another customer.

Garrick's guests were always taken to pay homage in the Temple, and were encouraged to write verses in Shakespeare's honour, which, if good enough, sometimes appeared anonymously in the London journals – the private cult became another subtle piece of publicity.

When it came to the British Museum in 1823 the statue stood first in the entrance hall and later on the main staircase, before being placed in its present position in the King's Library; all these backgrounds unfortunately proved less harmonious than the setting for which it was originally designed.

The Stratford Jubilee

G arrick also organized a more public demonstration of his Shakespeare worship. As the culmination of his campaign to popularize Shakespeare, the Stratford-upon-Avon Jubilee of 1769 arose almost accidentally; but here as usual Garrick was quick to seize an opportunity to arouse the widest possible enthusiasm and interest in a project dear to his heart. To regard the events of that summer at Stratford merely as an attempt by Garrick at self-glorification is wrong. There is no doubt that, while he could profit from reflected glory, Garrick genuinely loved and admired Shakespeare's works. Thus when the opportunity arose, he decided that when the theatres were closed during the summer he would stage a formal tribute, the first festival of its kind, and perhaps convince an even wider audience that Shakespeare was pre-eminent among dramatists.

The celebrations arose because the council at Stratford-upon-Avon, then still a sleepy and rather old-fashioned little town, decided to rebuild its decayed town hall. Garrick had visited the town with Macklin in 1742 to pay homage to Shakespeare and had seen the famous mulberry tree in the garden of New Place. He must have had a fair idea that little would have changed there, when in December 1767 he received a letter containing an interesting proposal.

Garrick, of course, knew that Shakespeare's mulberry tree was no more. In 1756 the steady trickle of visitors coming to Stratford had proved too troublesome to the Reverend Francis Gastrell, the owner of Shakespeare's

14 *Mulberry wood casket carved by Thomas Davies 1769. 5.5 × 8.6 × 5.2 in. (British Museum. Dept. of Medieval and Later Antiquities)*

old home. He had annoyed the townsmen by having the tree felled at dead of night. Many of the logs were bought by an astute tradesman named Thomas Sharp, and the manufacture of relics began. In 1762 Garrick himself bought some of the wood and had an elaborately carved chair made to Hogarth's design. The mulberry wood trade continued to prosper exceedingly and mysteriously until 1799 when Sharp died. Meanwhile Gastrell, aggrieved by disputes with the town council about taxes, had New Place pulled down in 1759, and left Stratford for ever.

✳ Mulberry wood figured in the council's plans to ensnare Garrick. The town hall needed decorating, and who better to supply a statue or painting of Shakespeare than England's foremost Shakespearian actor? Francis Wheler, a local lawyer acting on the council's behalf, wrote with a tempting offer. Garrick was asked to provide a suitable portrait for the new hall, where it would hang together with his own portrait, the two linked for posterity. In addition the corporation proposed to send Garrick the freedom of the borough contained in a mulberry wood casket [14–15]. The offer was eagerly accepted.

15 Back panel of the casket depicting Garrick as King Lear

✳The casket, now preserved in the Department of Medieval and Later Antiquities, British Museum, together with the document conferring on Garrick the freedom of Stratford, was carved by Thomas Davies of Birmingham, a skilled craftsman who took four months to complete the task. The elaborate and largely allegorical design represents Shakespeare and the three Graces on the front; symbols of tragedy and comedy appear on the ends [16], and the back depicts Garrick as King Lear, after the dramatic painting by Benjamin Wilson.

The idea of some form of public celebration at the opening of the town hall may actually have been suggested by the jovial actor and entertainer George Alexander Stevens, who visited the town at about this time; but it was Garrick who set about organizing the event. Hard upon newspaper accounts of the presentation of the freedom, which did not take place until May 1769, came the first announcements of the Jubilee to be held at the beginning of September. The publicity campaign, fed over three months both by tributes and many satirical attacks, rivals anything devised by modern advertising agents. Garrick is even accused of deliberately provoking the hostile comment to sustain the press reports and thus to arouse the interest of the whole country, but there were plenty of satirists ready to seize such a good opportunity.

16 *Side panel of the casket representing Tragedy, drawn by W. H. Brooke c. 1840*

Garrick, a born organizer, entered wholeheartedly into preparations in London, whilst his brother George laboured inefficiently in Stratford. Garrick wrote the *Ode* for the presentation and most of the songs to be performed during the celebrations; he engaged members of his London company for the procession of Shakespearian characters and to paint decorations and arrange firework displays. When local craftsmen proved insufficient for the task, he sent down a band of carpenters from London to construct the octagonal rotunda [17], modelled on that at the Ranelagh pleasure gardens, on the bank of the Avon, where most of the important events and balls during the three-day celebrations were to take place.

The criticism is justly made that none of Shakespeare's works was performed, and barely a line by him was quoted at the Jubilee. We must remember, however, that the event being commemorated was nominally the opening of the town hall and that there was no regularly accepted pattern for such celebrations. The Jubilee had many later imitations. There was no theatre in Stratford and no tradition of the major companies performing in the open air. Had it not rained, there would have been the large open air procession of Shakespearian characters, which would probably have better suited the mass of the local people; but it has been pointed out that if it had taken place the costumes might have appeared tawdry and shabby without the theatrical illusion of candlelight. Garrick's *Ode on Dedicating a Building*, however mediocre, when spoken against appropriate music by Thomas Arne was at least comparatively original, and with Garrick's moving delivery, supremely affecting. In their enthusiasm a number of his audience succeeded in breaking the hastily constructed benches in the rotunda.

The events of the Jubilee are now reasonably well known. Garrick acted as Steward [2] and host with a large medallion, suspended from a multicoloured ribbon, also carved by Davies, and a wand of office, both of mulberry wood. The first day went well and established a convivial atmosphere among the large audience, helped by the cheerful songs in *Shakespeare's Garland*, which were performed round the town and sung in a concert by the company after dinner. Nevertheless the fashionable crowd drawn from London and from miles around by the twin reputations of Shakespeare and Garrick had to stay in uncomfortable and expensive lodgings, and their enjoyment did not survive the change in the weather. Torrential rain caused the cancellation of the procession [18] and washed out most of the firework displays and decorations. The Avon rose alarmingly to flood the banks surrounding the rotunda, so that those who attended the second, masked, ball had to wade through or be carried over expanses of mud to get to their beds at six in the morning. They had not dared leave in the dark. Garrick held the second day together almost single-handed with his performance of the *Ode*, and the remaining festivities faded away in damp confusion. For the horse race for the Jubilee Cup run on the third day the course was knee-deep in water.

'The resurrection of Shakespeare', as the Jubilee was called by one uncomprehending local inhabitant, was hardly the success Garrick hoped for. For a few minutes he held his audience by a command which gave him equal authority with his idol, but he never gained the support of the scholars for this attempt at popularization. His losses, when he assumed also the debts of the various backers, totalled £2,000. News of the Jubilee prompted

17 The rotunda on the bank of the Avon. Contemporary engraving from 'The Gentleman's Magazine' 1769

18 An imaginary impression by James Saunders of the cancelled procession: the statue of Shakespeare arriving at the rotunda. Engraving by S. Ireland 1795

Sketch of Stratford Jubilee Booth or Amphitheatre.

Stratford Jubilee.

some similar celebrations abroad and influenced the awakening German romantic interest in Shakespeare; modern Stratford-upon-Avon can trace much of its development and probably its Shakespeare Memorial Theatre, built a century later almost on the site of the rotunda, to Garrick's anticipation of its annual Shakespeare festival.

In the event, the occasion did not prove an irremediable loss to Garrick either. Once the season opened at Drury Lane he staged the *Ode* before equally enraptured audiences, in the meantime turning the events and even the critics of the Jubilee into a spectacular entertainment which was performed one hundred and fifty-three times in three seasons; it received more performances than any Shakespeare play during his twenty-nine years as a manager. *The Jubilee* had as its centrepiece a magnificent mounting of the cancelled procession of characters. A few comic interludes were strung together round the successful songs, and the climax was a brilliant scene using a transparency, with the company paying homage to Shakespeare's statue.

Garrick the Actor

O nce a play is over it is impossible, even now with the help of films and records, to recreate the total effect of an actor's performance. We have to piece together Garrick's command of his art from a multitude of published accounts, and the result can never be entirely satisfactory.

Himself a dramatist and theatre manager, Henry Fielding, in the introduction to book seven of *Tom Jones* said that he regarded Garrick 'in tragedy to be the greatest genius the world hath ever produced', whilst Dr Johnson maintained that he preferred him in comedy. This was the only real dispute about Garrick's supremacy as an actor. A few actors challenged comparison with him in individual roles, and there were some parts like Othello which were outside his compass and which he soon abandoned; but, within his versatile range, from the mean, contemptible Abel Drugger and the boorish Sir John Brute [19] to Macbeth and Lear, Garrick was unrivalled.

Early eighteenth-century theatres in London were comparatively small. When Garrick first acted at Drury Lane it was little different from when Wren designed it in 1674. Although as manager he had the auditorium remodelled in 1762, and eventually increased the seating to eighteen hundred, the actors seemed nearer to their audiences, the front of the forestage being only twenty-five feet from the front boxes and gallery.

Some use could be made of facial expression, in which Garrick excelled. On the other hand lighting, depending

MR GARRICK *in the Character of* SʳJohn Brute *in the* Provok'd Wife
Done from an Original Picture of the same size, in the Possession of Her
Grace the Dutchess of Northumberland.

Printed for R. Sayer Nº 53 in Fleet Street, & J. Smith, Nº 35 Cheapside 1769. 2

19 Garrick as Sir John Brute in 'The Provok'd Wife' by Vanbrugh. Engraving after Johann Ludwig Fäsch 1769

20 Garrick as King Lear. Engraving by G. Terry 1779

on candles and reflectors, was still primitive and thus obscured any over-subtle effects. The actors had to rely principally on their voices and the use of broad gesture and movement. The few really detailed accounts of Garrick's acting, usually written by foreign observers, have by their very detail suggested an unduly slow, exaggerated and stagey effect in their accounts of the various movements. We know from the prompter John Brownsmith's *Dramatic Time-piece* of 1767 that a performance of *Hamlet* was calculated to last 2 hours 39 minutes, *King Lear* 2 hours 34 minutes and *Othello* 2 hours 23 minutes. However much the texts were cut, the performances must have run swiftly. The less analytical accounts of Garrick's acting usually emphasize his seeming naturalness, although the keener critics were well aware that this was achieved by finely calculated preparation and technique. There is a familiar account of how Garrick obtained ideas for some of the most moving scenes in his performance as Lear [20] by visiting a man who had gone mad when he accidentally killed his own child. Nor was Garrick above using mechanical effects to heighten the illusion. It is said that his chair in the closet

Mr Garrick as King Lear.

Blow winds and burst your Cheeks.

Act 3.^d Scene 1.st

Terry, sculp.^t

Publish'd by Harrison & C.º May 1, 1779.

MR GARRICK in the Character of HAMLET
Act I. Scene 4.th

Printed for R. Sayer, N.53, Fleet Street, & J. Smith, N.35, Cheapside, 16 Oct.r 1769. 5

21 *Garrick as Hamlet. Engraving after Johann Ludwig Fäsch 1769*

scene in *Hamlet* was weighted so that it invariably fell over when he started up on seeing the ghost. Henry Fielding's well-known description of Garrick's Hamlet in *Tom Jones*, as seen through the eyes of the naive Partridge, shows perfectly his power of utterly convincing the uncritical. The German philosopher Georg Christoph Lichtenberg, describing the same scene [21] still more objectively, affirms his extraordinary power: 'His whole demeanour is so expressive of terror that it made my flesh creep even before he began to speak.'

The actor's voice is one of his most powerful tools, but the many descriptions of Garrick speaking help us very little, although we have as full an account as the eighteenth century could provide. We are told that Garrick used his pleasant natural voice without straining it, that it

34

SINCE writing the foregoing treatife, I have heard Mr. Garrick in the character of Hamlet; and the principal differences that I can remember, between his manner, and what I have marked in the treatife, are as follow:

In the firft place, that fpeech, or foliloque, which I (for want of better judgement) have noted in the ftile of a ranting actor, fwelled with *forte* and foftened with *piano*, he delivered with little or no diftinction of piano and forte, but nearly uniform; fomething below the ordinary force, or, as a mufician would fay, *fotto voce*, or *fempre poco piano*.

Secondly, as to meafure, the firft line thus:

| 3 | To | be | | or | not to be | | | that is the | queftion. |

Thirdly, as to accent and quantity, thus:

| | To | die, | | — | to | fleep, | — | no | more. |

The words, *as flefh is heir to!* he pronounced as I have marked them in my variation, page 46.; where the two fyllables, *heir to*, are both acuted, and by that modulation, give the idea of the fenfe

22 *Transcription of Garrick's delivery of Hamlet's lines by Joshua Steele 1775*

was melodious and distinct even at its softest and that it was as expressive as his face. Various accounts attack details of his pronunciation. Dr John Hill, among other things a disappointed playwright, writes to complain that Garrick pronounces 'earth' to rhyme with 'worth' as we do now and speaks of 'furm' and 'vurtue'. Clearly he used on the whole the more modern eighteenth-century pronunciation. The phonetician Joshua Steele experimented with an original method using symbols to record the 'melody and measure', that is, the intonation and rhythm of speech, and he discussed his theories with Garrick. In *An essay towards establishing the melody and measure of speech, to be expressed and perpetuated by peculiar symbols,* 1775, he has left us a full transcription of 'To be or not to be' in an hypothetical actor's performance. Steele follows this by describing the more noticeable variations in Garrick's rendering [22], which he afterwards heard. If we allow for the fact that Garrick delivered the speech *sotto voce*, we have the closest possible record of his delivery, if not of his accent.

Garrick and Shakespeare's Plays

With the reopening of the theatres after the Restoration in 1660 plays by Shakespeare immediately returned to the stage, but often in versions altered and 'improved' beyond recognition to suit contemporary taste. The 'rough' lines were polished and emasculated, tragedies given happy endings, and comedies turned into operas and masques. In the early eighteenth century, scholars were beginning to interest themselves in producing editions of the full text of the plays, but these were seen as too barbarous for stage performance. Audiences and actors alike preferred the versions by William Davenant, Nahum Tate and Colley Cibber to which they were accustomed, and were as indifferent to what Shakespeare had actually written as they were to authenticity of costume. The actors and managers performed what they considered would be theatrically most effective, and made their adaptations accordingly.

Garrick had set himself up as Shakespeare's champion; and although to some extent he still operated in the old tradition – he appeared in corrupt versions of the plays and himself altered and rewrote others – it has been shown by George Winchester Stone and other modern scholars that he made considerable efforts to restore the original text.

Because the version was found to be supremely effective dramatically, throughout his acting career Garrick continued to play Richard III as the arch-villain of Colley Cibber's *The tragical history of King Richard III*; a play containing scenes taken from *King Henry VI,* as well as wholesale rewriting.

Garrick was responsible for inserting a procession into *Romeo and Juliet* and an additional scene where Juliet awakes to find Romeo not dead, but dying. Garrick always died most affectingly, and here, as in the mediocre dying speech he wrote for Macbeth, he was giving himself greater opportunities to demonstrate his art. Although *Macbeth* [23] still contained some of Davenant's lines and cheerful songs for the witches, in his acting version produced in 1744 and published in 1773 in Bell's edition of Shakespeare, Garrick restored line after line

23 *Garrick as Macbeth. Engraving after Johann Ludwig Fäsch 1769*

Mr. GARRICK in the Character of MACBETH.
Done from an Original picture of the same size in the Possession of her Grace the Dutchess of Northumberland.
printed for R. Sayer Nº 53 Fleet Street & J. Smith Nº 35 Cheapside. 1769.   7

Towards encreafing a FUND; for the Relief of thofe who from
their Infirmities fhall be obliged to retire from the Stage.

At the Theatre Royal in Drury-Lane,

This prefent THURSDAY, May 30, 1776,

H A M L E T.

(With A L T E R A T I O N S.)

Hamlet by Mr. GARRICK,

(Being the laft Time of his performing that Character)

King by Mr. JEFFERSON,

Ghoft Mr. BRANSBY, Horatio Mr. PACKER,

Polonius by Mr. BADDELEY,

Laertes by Mr. AICKIN,

Rofencraus by Mr. DAVIES, Guildenftern by Mr. FAWCETT,
Marcellus Mr. Wrighten, Player King Mr. Ufher, Lucianus Mr. Parfons,
Meffenger by Mr. Wright, Bernardo by Mr. Griffiths, Francifco by Mr. Nortis,

Queen by Mrs. HOPKIN,

Player Queen by Mrs. JOHNSTON,

Ophelia by Mrs. SMITH.

End of the Play, The Grand GARLAND DANCE,

By Mr. SLINGSBY,

Signor COMO, Signora CRESPI,

And Signora PACINI.

With an Occafional EPILOGUE to be fpoken by

Mr. GARRICK.

To which (by Defire) will be added

The DEUCE is in HIM.

Prattle by Mr. KING,
Colonel Tamper Mr. PALMER, Major Belford Mr. PACKER,
Madam Florival by Mrs. DAVIES, Bell by Mifs HOPKINS,
Emily by Mrs. KING.

Pit and Boxes are laid together; and no Admittance into the Pit or Boxes but with Tickets.
Ladies and Gentlemen are defired to come early, to prevent Confufion, and great inconvenience
t themfelves; Servants muft be at the Theatre by Five o'Clock to keep the Places.
The Doors will be opened at Half after Five.   To begin at Half after Six.

On Saturday, Mr. GARRICK will perform a principal Part

of Shakespeare's vigorous imagery in place of Davenant's heavy paraphrases. He is also known to have consulted the contemporary scholarly editions for the latest readings.

King Lear continued to be performed with a happy ending, because Garrick knew well the limits of innovation, and even Dr Johnson agreed that the tragic climax was too terrible to be borne. Garrick first performed *The history of King Lear* in Nahum Tate's version in 1742. The evidence suggests that from then on more and more of Shakespeare's lines were gradually restored. In 1756 a performance was announced 'with restorations from Shakespeare', and a prompt-book recently purchased by the British Library shows this process taking place. Garrick's first published performing text, in Bell's edition of Shakespeare in 1773, cuts sweepingly from Tate but restores enough Shakespearian lines to add 255 to the total. An edition published in 1786 as 'altered . . . by David Garrick' contains fifty further lines by Shakespeare. Garrick did not remove the love affair between Edgar and Cordelia nor restore the Fool, and he retained the ending demanded by poetic justice, which so easily reduced his audience to tears. George Colman in a rival version does not allow Edgar and Cordelia to be united, but to his contemporaries this seemed less fitting. Garrick again proved the accuracy of his judgment of public taste and the correct text was not performed until 1838.

Garrick's celebrated version of *Hamlet* [24] has received very severe criticism, but the version staged in 1772 contained in its early acts about 629 Shakespearian lines not heard for years, and enriched the parts of all the actors. It is true that, strongly influenced by the writings of Voltaire and other French critics, who convinced him that drama should not violate the rules of decorum, Garrick removed the gravediggers and Osric. Furthermore, he made sweeping changes to the last act, leaving an innocent Laertes and a mad Gertrude alive. Perhaps the comic gravedigger had been given too much prominence in earlier eighteenth-century productions, and Garrick's performance was enthralling enough to carry his audience without any comic relief; but,

24 *Playbill for Garrick's last performance as Hamlet in his own version of the play 1776*

although popular with audiences in his lifetime, this version did not long hold the stage after Garrick's death.

His version of *The Taming of the Shrew* survived into the nineteenth century. Previously a travesty called *Sauny the Scot* had been performed, but Garrick, largely by cutting the Christopher Sly and other early scenes, turned Shakespeare's play into a three-act comedy called *Catharine and Petruchio*, which at least gave the audience the rudiments of the original. Less successful is his *Florizel and Perdita,* based only on the two final acts of *The Winter's Tale*, which was performed at the same time.

As well as these, Garrick revived a number of Shakespeare's plays which had not been staged for many years. He himself made a version of *Cymbeline* and produced *Two Gentlemen of Verona* and a poor version of *Timon of Athens*. The ill success of two revivals which he was determined to stage shows that Garrick's appreciation of the dramatic and imaginative qualities of some of Shakespeare's plays was well in advance of that of his audiences. In 1758 he enlisted the help of the Shakespearian scholar Edward Capell in preparing a performing version of *Antony and Cleopatra,* which had not been staged since 1606. The text was cut and rearranged, but there were no significant additions. Despite new costumes and scenery, when the play was presented in January 1759 its reception was not enthusiastic, presumably because Dryden's *All for Love*, a more disciplined classical reworking of the story, although no longer much performed, was still preferred; but perhaps also because Antony was an expansive and grandiloquent part just beyond Garrick's range.

Similarly Garrick's attempt to stage a full version of *A Midsummer Night's Dream* resulted in total failure, for which he was not wholly to blame. Earlier in the century parts of the play had been performed as operas or burlesques, and in 1755 Garrick had presented it as an opera, *The Fairies,* with reasonable success. In 1763, while he went on his continental tour, George Colman, managing the theatre in his absence, was left to stage the new production. Surviving manuscript additions to the performing text show Garrick's bid to make the play

25 Manuscript additions by Garrick to 'A Midsummer Night's Dream' 1763

appeal more to contemporary taste, with added songs and comic scenes[25], but the survival in the Folger Shakespeare Library of the printed copy in which he made most of the alterations enables us to see that many more changes were made, presumably by Colman, before the play was published and performed. These and the poor acting, combined with the audience's dislike of the lovers' scenes, damned the piece, and Colman was left to salvage another operatic afterpiece, called *A Fairy Tale*, which was played with moderate success.

Garrick performed some nineteen Shakespearian parts in his career and staged some twenty-four of the plays (together with two by Ben Jonson) in versions of varying quality. By his performances in roles such as Benedick and Romeo, as well as his major tragic parts, he helped to inspire scholars to give the plays and their texts serious consideration and won the allegiance of audiences to the regular performance of Shakespeare's plays.

Garrick as Author

The author of some twenty-two new plays, in addition to adaptations and a great deal of light occasional verse, Garrick has no great claim to literary originality: he wrote to a required formula to serve an immediate need.

He did not usually invent the plots for his plays. As manager he accurately anticipated what new pieces were needed each season and what would suit his audiences. Most of his plays are afterpieces, the two-act light comedies which followed the full five-act mainpiece on each day's playbill. These lasted less well and a considerable number were needed each season. Garrick, helped no doubt by his Huguenot descent, read French fluently and turned to contemporary dramatists in Paris for suitable ideas for plots, although his characters are entirely English. His afterpieces, like *The Lying Valet,* 1741, *Miss in her Teens,* 1747 [26], and the rather sentimental *The Guardian,* 1759, are lively comedies of situation and character, containing a fair amount of social satire, and were usually well received, whether or not Garrick played in them himself.

His best-known play, the five-act *The Clandestine Marriage* 1766 [27], is one of the few plays in the century to approach the standard of Goldsmith's and Sheridan's great comedies and it is still occasionally performed. As it was written in collaboration with George Colman, each author deserves some of the credit for the play's great success. Disputes about their respective contributions have been largely settled by an examination of the

On my Words[.] he is a Bully

We shall certainly be one another a Prejudice

The celebrated fig

26 The duel from
Garrick's comedy
'Miss in her
Teens' c.1747.
Garrick, on the
left, plays Fribble

surviving manuscript in the Folger Shakespeare Library,
which shows that Garrick wrote at least half the play,
most materially the scenes involving the ridiculous Lord
Ogleby, and generally tightened the construction. The

I shall annihilate the Nothingg of your Soul & Body

Is all your fury gone Mr. Flash

Scene in Miss in her Teens.

old fop, brilliantly characterized by Thomas King in the
original production, was the one part which at the end of
his career Garrick wished he himself had played. It is
generally assumed that this time Garrick invented the

THE

Clandeſtine Marriage,

A

COMEDY.

As it is ACTED at the

Theatre-Royal in *Drury-Lane.*

BY

GEORGE COLMAN

AND

DAVID GARRICK.

Hac adhibe vultus, et in unâ parce duobus :
Vivat, et ejuſdem ſimus uterque parens !   OVID.

LONDON:

Printed for T. BECKET and P. A. DE HONDT, in the Strand ;
R. BALDWIN, in Pater-noſter-Row ; R. DAVIS, in Pic-
cadilly ; and T. DAVIES, in Ruſſel-Street, Covent-
Garden.

M.DCC.LXVI.

27 Garrick's best known play, written in collaboration with George Colman 1766

basic plot, and it was considered original and amusing enough to form the basis for Cimarosa's lively opera *Il matrimonio segreto* in 1792. Compared with Lord Ogleby, however, the opera's oddly named Count Robinson is a disappointing figure.

Other plays of Garrick's were written merely as vehicles for the display of the scenery, costumes, singing, dancing and special effects expected of a Christmas entertainment. *Lilliput,* written for a company of children in 1756, *Cymon,* 1767, and *A Christmas Tale,* 1773, are examples of this type of work; the third proving the vehicle for one of the most magnificent achievements of the great theatrical painter, de Loutherbourg. It is difficult now to imagine that their vapid plots and thin verse were very entertaining; but the first two survived

with alterations into the nineteenth century, and *Cymon*
was remembered well enough to be considered worth
burlesquing by J. R. Planché as late as 1850.

These plays contain a great deal of music, and although
Garrick himself had no ear, he possessed a happy facility
in writing rhythmical and melodious verses which he was
prepared to pay the best contemporary composers, Arne,
Boyce, and Dibdin to set, and which became popular
songs. *Heart of oak,* inserted into his spectacular *Harlequin's Invasion* (which shows Shakespeare triumphing
over Harlequin), is perhaps his most widely known work,
although not many people today remember who wrote
the words for William Boyce.

Garrick's greatest claim to literary excellence comes

*28 One of Garrick's
occasional poems,
printed on Horace
Walpole's private
press at Strawberry
Hill 1757*

T O

Mr. G R A Y,

ON HIS

O D E S.

I.

REPINE not, GRAY, that our weak dazzled Eyes
  Thy daring heights and brightnefs fhun,
How few can track the Eagle to the fkies,
  Or like Him, gaze upon the Sun !

II.

The gentle Reader loves the gentle Mufe,
  That little dares, and little means,
Who humbly fips her Learning from *Reviews*,
  Or flutters in the *Magazines*.

III.

No longer now from Learning's facred Store
  Our Minds their health and vigor draw;
HOMER, and PINDAR are rever'd no more,
  No more the *Stagyrite is Law*.

IV.

from his many theatrical prologues and epilogues. He wrote other topical verse, one piece of which, *To Mr. Gray on his Odes* [28], was actually printed in a limited edition on Horace Walpole's private press at Strawberry Hill; there are also longer satires, but he knew his audiences well, and his lively wit and facility in couplets were ideally suited to charming and cajoling them into the right mood.

James Boswell, who was, of course, apt to flatter, said of a letter he received from Garrick in 1774: 'It was a pine-apple of finest flavour'. A massive amount of Garrick's correspondence, which he himself selected for preservation, survives in the Forster Collection in the Victoria and Albert Museum. As well as containing Garrick's draft letters illustrating most aspects of his life and career, it supplies a fascinating picture of his relationships with practically everyone of note in eighteenth-century England, and with many in France as well. The range of his acquaintances and friends is very fully demonstrated.

Unfortunately no letters survive between Garrick and his oldest friend Samuel Johnson [29]. The relationship between them was complex. Garrick respected and a little feared his formidable former master and was always anxious for his approval; but he was also prepared to mimic him for the young Burneys. Garrick staged Johnson's play *Irene* in 1749; and Johnson had earlier agreed to write the great prologue [30] for the opening of Garrick's first season as manager in 1747. In this Garrick proclaimed his allegiance to Shakespeare but also defined perfectly his own and the theatre's dependence upon their audience:

The drama's laws the drama's patrons give,
For we that live to please, must please to live.

It seems reasonably clear that Johnson was jealous of his friend's quick worldly success in comparison with his own years of literary drudgery before he achieved recognition, and occasional peevishness appears in his comments about 'Davy'. It was not until 1772 that Garrick was allowed to be elected to the famous Literary

29 *Dr Samuel Johnson. Mezzotint by S. W. Reynolds after Sir Joshua Reynolds*

48

r Joshua Reynolds Pinx.ᵗ   S W Reynolds Scu

DR JOHNSON.

PROLOGUE

SPOKEN BY

Mr GARRICK.

HEN Learning's Triumph o'er her bar-b'rous Foes

First rear'd the Stage, immortal SHAKE-SPEAR rose ;

Each Change of many-colour'd Life he drew,

Exhausted Worlds, and then imagin'd new :

Exi-

30 The beginning of the 'Prologue . . . at the Opening of the Theatre in Drury-Lane 1747' by Samuel Johnson

Club. However, Boswell and Sir Joshua Reynolds in his *Johnson on Garrick* were among those who noticed that, while Johnson would chide and criticize Garrick quite severely himself, he did not allow others this privilege and would immediately come to Garrick's defence. He was overcome with grief at Garrick's funeral and would not fill the vacant place at the Club for a year. When he died in 1785 few better places could have been found for his grave in Westminster Abbey than by the side of his friend.

Garrick and the Visual Arts

G arrick's commission from Roubiliac is a notable example of his patronage of the major artists working in eighteenth-century London. His statue of Shakespeare for Stratford-upon-Avon was an improved version of Scheemakers' monument in Westminster Abbey, suitably cast in lead for an outdoor site by John Cheere, the pioneer of mass production in sculpture. Garrick sat for busts by Roubiliac and Nollekens.

The exhibition devoted to Johann Zoffany at the National Portrait Gallery in 1977 demonstrated most effectively how Garrick discovered and employed Zoffany to their mutual advantage. Garrick had been an admirer and patron of Hogarth, who had begun the tradition of a new type of genre painting in England showing scenes from plays in performance. As well as painting and engraving his magnificent dramatic portrait of Garrick as Richard III, Hogarth also drew him as the farmer [31] in his topical sketch, *The Farmer's Return*, 1762, and this appeared as the frontispiece to the published text. Hogarth also painted an attractive private portrait of Mr and Mrs Garrick, which was unfinished at his death in 1764. Garrick wrote the epitaph for Hogarth's tomb at Chiswick.

Garrick purchased from Hogarth the series of four robust election paintings which now hang in Sir John Soane's Museum. The artist, despairing of a sale, had organized a lottery to dispose of them when Garrick bought them to hang in the Bow room at Hampton,

The Farmer's Return.

W.ᵐ Hogarth delin.   James Basire Sculp.

*31 Garrick in his
interlude 'The
Farmer's Return'.
Engraving by
J. Basire after
William Hogarth
1762*

just as Zoffany's two tranquil conversation pieces set on the riverside lawns at Hampton [32], hung in the Adam dining room in the Adelphi. (The drawing room is preserved at the Victoria and Albert Museum, together with some of the Garricks' Chinese bedroom furniture from Hampton.)

Johann Zoffany was largely Garrick's discovery. He rescued the young man from his menial post as drapery painter in Benjamin Wilson's studio, took him off to Hampton in 1762 to paint his enchanting domestic studies, and conceived the plan of using the engravings which could be made of theatrical portraits to publicize his London productions. The aggrieved Benjamin Wilson like the scene painter at Drury Lane, Francis Hayman, had painted the younger Garrick in a number of over-dramatic canvases, but he was outclassed in this genre by Zoffany. Although Zoffany's paintings were composed in the studio and the figures probably painted one by one as the actors had time to pose in costume, they suggest, at their most successful, the vivid interactions of an actual performance. The mezzotints published from these originals were widely collected and enhanced the fame of both Garrick and Zoffany.

In his private persona Garrick sat for many of the major painters of his day, both in England and abroad. Reynolds, who knew him well, was less successful at portraying him than Gainsborough, who has left a portrait, now in the National Portrait Gallery [33],

32 Mr and Mrs Garrick and the Shakespeare temple at Hampton 1762. Painting by Johann Zoffany. The statue can just be seen through the doorway (Lord Lambton)

33 *Garrick c.1770.*
Painting by
Thomas
Gainsborough
(National
Portrait Gallery)

which conveys his charm and humour if not his anima-
tion. Gainsborough also painted the full-length portrait
bought by the corporation of Stratford to hang in the
town hall beside Benjamin Wilson's portrait of Shakespeare which Garrick had presented. Gainsborough had
turned down this part of the commission. Garrick was
appropriately portrayed leaning against a bust of
Shakespeare as presiding deity. Mrs Garrick thought the
painting a good likeness and it is most unfortunate that
it was destroyed by fire in 1946.

It seems strange that Garrick's afterpiece *Lethe*, a
slight little piece of topical social satire, should inspire
so much artistic activity. It was first staged on 15th
April 1740, before Garrick's debut, and was undoubtedly

written to suit the leading actors in the Drury Lane company. A series of contemporary types are paraded in a mythological setting – an idea not new, but based on Vanbrugh's *Aesop*. The attractive songs by Thomas Arne undoubtedly contributed to the play's popularity; and, although afterpieces were often not published at this date, *Lethe* proved so successful with audiences that it gained the dubious distinction of an abbreviated pirated edition published in 1745 before the first authorized one in 1749.

Garrick's cast varied over the years more than the published editions suggest, but the play took its established form in 1756 when he wrote for himself the highly successful part of Lord Chalkstone [34], the forerunner of the magnificent old fop Lord Ogleby in *The Clandestine Marriage*. Zoffany painted Garrick as Chalkstone and

M.ͬGARRICK in the Character of Lord Chalkstone.
in LETHE.
Printed for Rob.ᵗSayer N.º53 Fleet Street. & Jn.ºSmith N.º35 Cheapside.

34 Garrick as Lord Chalkstone in his play 'Lethe'. Engraving after Johann Ludwig Fäsch

other engravings were in turn derived from this. From these engravings was designed an attractive cotton and linen wall-hanging in blue and white (preserved in the Victoria and Albert Museum), perhaps in connection with a Command Performance of the play in 1766, [35–36] which was also attended by Jean-Jacques Rousseau.

Particularly interesting, however, is the even earlier use of characters from the play as models for Bow porcelain figures. Kitty Clive made the part of Mrs Riot, the 'modern fine lady', very much her own, and indeed played it at her final performance in 1769. Henry Woodward excelled as debonair young men and was

35 Playbill for performances of 'Zara' and 'Lethe' 1758

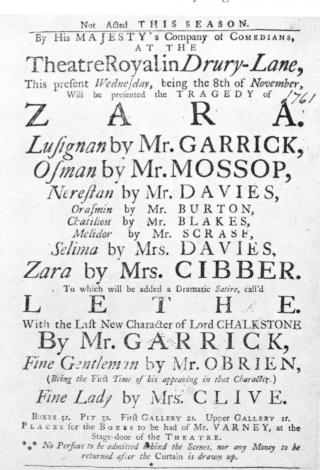

Not Acted THIS SEASON.

By His MAJESTY's Company of COMEDIANS,
AT THE

TheatreRoyalin *Drury-Lane*,

This present *Wednesday*, being the 8th of *November*, *1761*
Will be presented the TRAGEDY of

Z A R A.

Lusignan by Mr. GARRICK,
Osman by Mr. MOSSOP,
Nerestan by Mr. DAVIES,
Orasmin by Mr. BURTON,
Chatilion by Mr. BLAKES,
Melidor by Mr. SCRASE,
Selima by Mrs. DAVIES,
Zara by Mrs. CIBBER.

To which will be added a Dramatic *Satire*, call'd

L E T H E.

With the Last New Character of Lord CHALKSTONE

By Mr. GARRICK,

Fine Gentleman by Mr. OBRIEN,
(Being the First *Time* of *his appearing in that Character*.)

Fine Lady by Mrs. CLIVE.

BOXES 5s. PIT 3s. First GALLERY 2s. Upper GALLERY 1s.
PLACES for the BOXES to be had of Mr. VARNEY, at the Stage-door of the THEATRE.
** No Persons to be admitted behind the Scenes, nor any Money to be returned after the Curtain is drawn up.

To-morrow, *KING HENRY the Eighth*, and the *Diversions of the Morning* by Mr. FOOTE.

equally successful as the Beau or 'modern fine gentleman'. Francis Hayman, the scene-painter at Drury Lane, made a drawing of Woodward in his role, which was afterwards published as an undated mezzotint by J. McArdell, and Charles Mosley published an engraving of Kitty Clive in character in 1750, which was sufficiently popular to reappear as a design for a watch-paper. These prints were the models for two of Thomas Frye's more ambitious figures [37] at his Bow porcelain works, confirming his successful development there of his process for English porcelain manufacture. One of the Kitty Clive figures bears the date 1750, with others undated; and the existence of at least three Kitty Clives made of a different porcelain body, containing no bone-ash, suggests that they achieved sufficient popularity to be worth pirating, perhaps at Derby. The Department of Medieval and

Mʳ GARRICK in the Character of LUSIGNAN in Zarah. Act. II.
London. Printed for J.Smith Nº 35 Cheapside & R. Sayer Nº 53 Fleet Street Sep.ᵗ 15 1770.

36 *Garrick as Lusignan in 'Zara' by Aaron Hill. Engraving after Johann Ludwig Fäsch 1770*

Later Antiquities, British Museum, owns, as well as finished examples, an unfinished Kitty Clive in the biscuit state on which the unglazed details appear with greater refinement. The figure lacks the left arm, which would have been moulded separately.

These evidences of *Lethe*'s success end on a sadder note. By George III's command, a solo reading of the play before the royal family at Windsor was Garrick's last public performance, in the spring of 1777, after his retirement from the stage. He took great pains with his delivery and revised the text, adding a new prologue and a new character, but naturally he did not receive the tumultuous applause he expected in the theatre, and was bitterly disappointed by the king's formal 'Very well'.

Lethe is only one example of the way in which artistic activity was inspired by the increasing popularity and respectability of the theatre. New publishing ventures in the 1770s, like Bell's *British Theatre* and Lowndes' *New English Theatre*, revived a fashion popular in the early years of the century for issuing individual plays with well-drawn and engraved frontispieces, in this case of an actor in character. These, and cheaper series produced for an even wider market, provided models for other craftsmen. A most attractive series of Liverpool tiles appeared, decorated with versions of these actors' portraits.

37 *Bow porcelain figure of Kitty Clive as Mrs Riot in 'Lethe' c.1750. 12.3 in. (British Museum. Dept. of Medieval and Later Antiquities)*

Garrick as a Book Collector

G arrick had by the time he died amassed a magnificent general library, rich in editions with engraved illustrations and in English and foreign, particularly French, literature.

In 1763, after going through a period of unpopularity with the public through difficulties at the theatre, he and his wife set off on a two-year continental tour which would take them to Italy, Germany and France. If on his return he was not welcomed as an actor, he planned to leave the stage forever. The journey was a typical Grand Tour, during which Garrick found himself lionized in many places abroad. Mrs Garrick suffered badly from a rheumatic complaint in Italy, but it was Garrick who suffered the more severe illness. He contracted some disease, possibly typhoid fever, in Italy, to which he succumbed in Munich, and for a week his life was in danger. After convalescence the Garricks, avoiding a visit to Voltaire at Ferney, travelled on to Paris, where they held court in their lodgings and made many friends, who enriched their correspondence in later years. Among the Paris friends was Jean Monnet, the theatrical impresario turned bookseller, who often sent Garrick consignments of French books, as did his Paris bankers. Similar parcels came from friends and agents in Italy.

The growing library was eventually housed in an impressive room on the ground floor of his house in the Adelphi, where, according to Noverre, Garrick received his visitors and conducted his business each morning. After his widow's death the library, which she had bought back from the nephew to whom it was bequeathed, took ten days to sell.

A special bookcase in the library was reserved for Garrick's collection of early English plays, which he started to form soon after his successful debut, when he was already earning a considerable salary and greatly interested in the history of the English drama. The books were probably bought from various sources and once his interest became known he also received some important gifts. Garrick always intended the collection for some public library in a learned institution, and his will provides: 'I give and bequeath ... all my collection of old English plays to the Trustees of the British Museum for the time being for the use of the publick'.

Garrick had friends among the London booksellers, including some like Paul Vaillant, Somerset Draper and Thomas Becket who were at various times his own publishers. These dealt also in second-hand books, and may well have supplied him. The author and bookseller Robert Dodsley had previously owned a number of the plays and had marked them up in ink for his *A Select Collection of Old Plays,* 1744.

In building up and organizing the collection Garrick took advantage of the expert knowledge of Edward Capell, the retiring, single-minded and rather touchy scholar who held the office of Deputy Inspector of Plays for the Lord Chamberlain. Capell is best known now for his painstaking and remarkably accurate edition of Shakespeare which anticipates modern standards of textual criticism. With this edition and the accompanying volumes of annotations in mind, he also collected plays on his own behalf and this collection was given to Trinity College, Cambridge. The initials E.C. appear on about thirty titlepages in the Garrick collection, and others have missing titlepages supplied in Capell's handwriting.

Capell was responsible for cataloguing and binding up Garrick's collection in what he describes as: 'A first essay; faulty and uncorrected', and indeed a modern librarian may shudder at Capell's complex and illogical arrangement. The plays were bound up in groups according to size, but the manuscript catalogue neither reflects this arrangement nor is it ordered either alphabetically by author or title, or by date of acquisition. The two interwoven sequences of primary copy and other editions of the same work make the numbering extremely confusing. The index of titles, itself in two sequences, always has to be consulted before the full entry can be found.

Garrick's collection contained some 1,300 plays and collected editions of plays published between 1510 and 1720, but is richest in works of the late sixteenth and seventeenth centuries [38]. There are some sixteen unique examples of works or editions and many other rare items

38 'The Spanish Tragedy' by Thomas Kyd c.1592. The only known copy of the first surviving edition

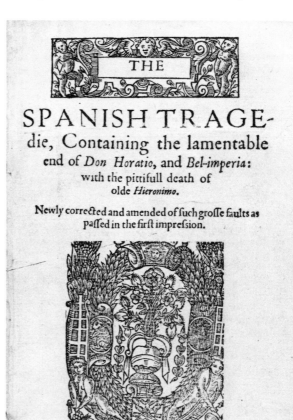

THE

SPANISH TRAGE-
die, Containing the lamentable
end of *Don Horatio*, and *Bel-imperia*:
with the pittifull death of
olde *Hieronimo*.

Newly corrected and amended of such grosse faults as
passed in the first impression.

AT LONDON
Printed by *Edward Allde*, for
Edward White.

significant in the history of the development of English drama. The plays can in some cases be traced back to earlier private collections like that of Lewis Theobald or the Harleian Library, for Garrick was not the first man to collect plays. Nevertheless his bequest to the new British Museum assured the preservation of most of these treasures for succeeding generations of scholars.

During his lifetime Garrick was always pleased to open his library to scholars or to send them parcels of books on loan. A fire was always to be lit for Samuel Johnson, if he came, although Johnson's constitutional indolence unfortunately prevented him from taking proper advantage of the offer while preparing his edition of Shakespeare. Other scholars like Richard Warner, Thomas Warton, Thomas Hawkins and Bishop Thomas Percy all ack-

39 'Hycke Scorner'
printed by Wynkyn
de Worde c.1515.
The earliest play
in Garrick's
collection

nowledged Garrick's help in supplying books. In return Warner gave Garrick three Shakespeare quartos; and, inspired by Bishop Percy, Thomas Astle the antiquary gave him a volume containing exceedingly rare and valuable early plays including *Hycke Scorner* [1515?] [39] and *Everyman* [1526?].

Since Garrick's death, his collection has suffered a number of misfortunes. When in 1780 his executors finally released the books it was discovered that some of the most valuable items, including the Shakespeare First Folio and the folio *Works* of Ben Jonson, had been retained by Mrs Garrick, who could not be persuaded to part with them. To the dismay of the Trustees both were sold with Garrick's other books in 1823.

At the time of the bequest there were almost no other plays in the Museum's collections. For many years the Garrick plays, still in their original arrangement, provided the most readily accessible collection for readers like Charles Lamb who were becoming aware of the riches of the Elizabethan and Jacobean age. Unfortunately they did not escape the depredations made by the sales of supposed duplicates from the Museum in 1788 and 1805, when many volumes were broken up in order to sell items, now irreplaceable, for a few shillings, which would barely cover the cost of rebinding. Some of the plays were transferred and exchanged with copies in other collections in the Library, and some were perfected with leaves from elsewhere. In the 1840s Sir Anthony Panizzi had the plays bound individually; a measure which has a little eased the problem of wear and tear. Each volume is stamped with Garrick's coat of arms in gold.

The latest blow to the collection came earlier this century through the marauding of the notorious T. J. Wise. David Foxon, a member of the Museum staff, in the early 1950s discovered that many leaves had been cut out to perfect copies sold to libraries in the United States or copies in Wise's own Ashley Library, which is fortunately now in the British Library.

A complete catalogue of the Garrick plays will shortly be published by the British Library, and in this the complicated history of the collection is described.

Garrick as Manager of Drury Lane Theatre,

his retirement and death

Garrick's greatest asset as a theatre manager was almost certainly his accurate judgment and uncanny anticipation of public taste. By selecting and revising plays that continued to please, he was able to establish the finances of Drury Lane on a sound basis. The audiences were drawn from a fairly small section of society, since seat prices were relatively high, and thus programmes had to be changed frequently to keep the houses filled. Theatregoers were eager for variety, but only within fairly narrow limits, and their tastes were insular. By the middle of the century they tended to prefer the pathetic in tragedy and the sentimental in comedy; and they had also a large appetite for insipid spectacular entertainments. While Garrick managed to satisfy these tastes he also contrived to insinuate a certain number of revivals of Elizabethan and Jacobean plays into his repertoire. He knew that by performing himself he could always raise the average takings and make up for losses, but during the later years of his career he was content to play fewer than thirty nights in the season and let his company and his excellent productions suffice for the rest.

James Lacy, Garrick's fellow patentee, attended efficiently to the financial side of the administration, and to the mechanics of productions, and the partnership worked very well. Lacy controlled the expenses carefully, and Garrick was undoubtedly careful too, as his early poverty had taught him thrift – a quality easily interpreted as meanness in the open-handed theatrical world. His many private benefactions were not publicized; sometimes those who had received help and loans, like the satirist Samuel Foote, themselves spread the rumours of his parsimony.

Garrick was a good organizer and his willingness to be accommodating helped enormously in his management of a company of temperamental actors and actresses. He was prepared to go to considerable lengths to satisfy their demands, but insisted on proper discipline.

Jean-Georges Noverre, the great choreographer and teacher of dancing, as well as leaving in his letters to Voltaire some graphic descriptions of Garrick's acting, singles out some of his virtues as a producer and director. Garrick insisted upon attendance at rehearsals, which he conducted himself and thus improved acting standards. He had fines levied for unpunctuality and other lapses. In return the actors were paid regularly and supported by good productions, scenery and costumes. Drury Lane Theatre was continually refurbished and modernized [40], and the seating capacity enlarged. In 1775 Garrick employed the Adam brothers to renovate and improve the public parts of the house. They also created a dignified classical façade on Bridges Street which only survived until Sheridan had it demolished in 1791.

Just as he always employed the best musicians to aid his dramatic effects, so also did Garrick seek out the best scene-painters for Drury Lane. The standard of stage settings improved greatly during his managership. This was partly due to the work of John French and the versatile Domenico Angelo, who among other effects produced magical coloured lights by means of coloured silk screens. Garrick himself obtained footlights and lamps during his second visit to Paris, but it was not until the teacher of his two experts, Philippe Jacques de Loutherbourg, came to London in 1771 that there was a startling and permanent improvement in theatrical lighting and scenery, and thence in heightened illusion. From 1773 de Loutherbourg was employed as scenic adviser at Drury Lane at the large salary of £500 a year; he is remembered for introducing dramatic top lighting, more naturalistic painted scenery, act drops, mechanical effects and costumes in harmony with the scenic designs.

THE
T H E A T R E S.
A
POETICAL DISSECTION.

By Sir N I C H O L A S N I P C L O S E, Baronet.

Suppofe JOB living 'midft the Critic train,
Our Theatres would ope his angry vein.

Behold the Mufes ROSCIUS sue in vain,
Taylors & Carpenters usurp their Reign.

L O N D O N:
PRINTED FOR JOHN BELL, IN THE STRAND, AND C. ETHERINGTON, AT YORK,
M.DCC.LXXII.

In return for the increased seating Garrick succeeded in abolishing the old custom of allowing the audience to pass freely behind the scenes, and indeed actually to sit on the stage to swell the actors' takings on their benefit nights.

Other attempts to reform audience behaviour were not so successful. Audiences were less inhibited than nowadays in showing their displeasure, just as their susceptibility to pathos and emotional effects seems to have been greater. Even allowing for some exaggeration, one often reads accounts of a whole audience moved to tears. However, if an audience for any reason disliked what was presented, it made such a noise and sometimes pelted the actors, so that they could not proceed. This happened to Garrick's only really disastrous venture, *The Chinese Festival*, in 1755. He imported a company of dancers from France and ordered expensive new scenery and costumes

40 *'The Theatres' by Francis Gentleman 1772, depicts Garrick preoccupied with his scenery*

67

FIZGIG.

in an attempt to rival Rich's pantomimes at Covent Garden, but hostile anti-French crowds drowned the music, and on the sixth night rioted and seriously damaged the theatre, before the performances were abandoned. The managers are thought to have lost £4,000. Garrick hoped to reduce the power of the mob by removing some of the more disruptive elements. It was the custom to admit anyone at half-price after the third act of the main piece of the evening, and this often introduced a rowdy element as well as greatly reducing the receipts. When in 1763 the two theatres together tried to abolish this practice, an old enemy of Garrick's, Thaddeus Fitzpatrick [41], whom he had satirized as Fizgig in his poem *The Fribbleriad*, 1761, an idle man about town and troublemaker, incited a crowd to raise a riot, causing considerable damage first at Drury Lane and later at Covent Garden. The managers had to capitulate and full prices could only be charged, as previously, for first nights or for pantomimes.

41 Thaddeus Fitzpatrick. Caricature as frontispiece to Garrick's attack on him 'The Fribbleriad' 1761

The actors, of course, continued to augment their salaries by their allotted benefit performances at the end of each season, and Garrick instituted a number of new benefits for charitable objects. Covent Garden was ahead of him in setting up a 'Decayed Actors' Fund', but Garrick immediately in 1765 set up a similar fund at Drury Lane and contributed over £4,000 to it over the years. In 1776 he paid for, and persuaded his friend Edmund Burke to see through Parliament, the Act regularizing the Theatrical Fund.

Just as the price riots were in part responsible for sending the Garricks off on their long continental tour in 1763–65, so by 1776 Garrick had become tired of the increasing worries of management. He was constantly solicited for favours and attacked by scores of disappointed authors whose plays were not a success, or were judged unlikely to succeed. Even those whose plays he had staged were not above attacking him and satirizing him maliciously in newspapers and anonymous pamphlets. In 1773 William Kenrick published a particularly scurrilous libel entitled *Love in the suds* involving Garrick with the playwright Isaac Bickerstaffe who had fled the

At the Theatre Royal in Drury-Lane,
This preſent MONDAY, June 10, 1776,

The WONDER.

Don Felix by Mr. GARRICK,
Col. Briton by Mr. SMITH,
Don Lopez by Mr BADDELEY,
Don Pedro by Mr. PARSONS,
Liſſardo by Mr. KING,
Frederick by Mr. PACKER,
Gibby by Mr. MOODY,
Iſabella by Miſs HOPKINS,
Flora by Mrs. WRIGHTEN,
Inis by Mrs. BRADSHAW,
Violante by Mrs. YATES.

End of Act I. The Grand GARLAND DANCE,
By Signor GIORGI, Mrs. SUTTON,
And Mr. SLINGSBY.

To which will be added a Muſical Entertainment, call'd

The WATERMAN.

The PRINCIPAL CHARACTERS by
Mr. BANNISTER,
Mr. DAVIES,
And Mr. DODD.
Mrs. WRIGHTEN,
And Mrs. JEWELL.

To conclude with the Grand Scene of The REGATTA.
Ladies are deſired to ſend their Servants a little after 5 to keep Places, to prevent Confuſion.
The Doors will be opened at HALF after FIVE o'Clock.
To begin at HALF after SIX o'Clock.   Vivant Rex & Regina.
The Profits of this Night being appropriated to the Benefit of
The Theatrical Fund, the Uſual Addreſs upon that Occaſion
Will be ſpoken by Mr. GARRICK, before the Play.

42 Playbill for Garrick's final performance as Don Felix in 'The Wonder' by Susanna Centlivre 1776

country to avoid prosecution for the capital crime of sodomy. The offensive work went through five editions before Kenrick was forced to issue a public apology. Since his illness in Germany, Garrick had often suffered bouts of ill health, and acting now tired him. After 1768 he did not create a new role; and he was exhausted by the increasing squabbles in his company particularly between his three jealous principal actresses. His fortune was already made and he was a considerable property owner, so that he could well afford to rest and enjoy a quiet country life. In 1776 he announced his decision to retire and, amid scenes of wild enthusiasm and emotion, appeared one by one in his great roles for the last time, his final performance being on 10th June [42] as Don Felix in Susanna Centlivre's *The Wonder*[43].

After prolonged negotiations Garrick's half share in the

Drury Lane patent had been sold for £35,000 to Richard Brinsley Sheridan [44], his father-in-law Thomas Linley and their backer Dr James Ford. Garrick did not at first entirely give up his connection with Drury Lane, but helped rehearse his old company in Sheridan's *The School for Scandal* in 1777 to bring about the perfectly balanced performance [45] which ensured its success. Garrick supplied the prologue for the occasion.

As days passed, however, he was seen less in London and spent the summer months travelling with Eva Maria to visit the country houses of the couple's many well-born friends. There they were always welcome, for both were excellent company. It was at Lord Palmerston's house at Broadlands in September 1778 that Garrick made his will, and at Althorp, the home of Earl Spencer, that he was taken seriously ill in January 1779. He and his wife

43 Garrick as Don Felix with Anne Barry as Donna Violante. Engraving after Johann Ludwig Fäsch 1769

44 Richard Brinsley Sheridan. Engraving after J. C. Lochee 1794

Mrs BARRY and Mr GARRICK.
in the Characters of Donna Violante and Don Felix in the Wonder.
Done from an Original Picture in the Possession of Her Grace
the Dutchess of Northumberland.
Printed for J. Smith No.35 in Cheapside & R. Sayer No.53 Fleet Street 1769.   3

Mrs Abingdon, Mr King, Mr Smith, and Mr Palmer, in the Characters of
Lady Teazle, Sir Peter Teazle, Charles and Joseph Surface,
in the Comedy of the School for Scandal.   Pub.d Oct.r 20.th 1778.

45 The screen scene from 'The School for Scandal' by Sheridan 1778. This is one of the few contemporary engravings that gives a clear impression of a play in performance

returned quickly to the Adelphi, but Garrick's condition deteriorated, and on 20th January he died peacefully aged not quite sixty-two.

The public character of Garrick's funeral on 1st February 1779 was probably due to Sheridan, who rode prominently in the procession as chief mourner and presumably acted as stage manager for the occasion. As was customary, engraved invitations were sent out and mourning rings given to friends; the scale of the procession suggests some exploitation, but the presence of crowds so large that mounted troops were needed to open a path through them also indicates the respect, admiration and affection in which the brilliant actor was held by the public at large. As Edmund Burke wrote: 'He raised the character of his profession to the rank of a liberal art'.

Garrick died an extremely wealthy man. His estate,

which was divided between his wife and relations, totalled at least £100,000. Mrs Garrick, enjoined by his will to preserve their two homes, settled calmly into an obscure, quiet and faithful widowhood of forty-three years. At first she went into society a little, occasionally visited the theatre and entertained large family parties, but in extreme old age she became more of a recluse and worried unduly about whether her income was sufficient to maintain the properties. She died on 16th October 1822 at the age of ninety-eight [46], and was buried beside her husband.

Garrick was not well served by his memorials. Sheridan wrote and staged at Drury Lane a monody [47] reminiscent of Garrick's Jubilee *Ode*. It was not great poetry, and was duly parodied by Leonard MacNally as: *The apotheosis of Punch . . . with a monody on the death of the late Master Punch.* A number of feeble allegorical engravings and verse tributes appeared. After a delay, in part due to the death of James Hickey, the sculptor originally chosen, in 1797 Garrick's executor Albany Wallis had a monument

46 *Mrs Garrick in 1820 aged 96. Etching by Robert Cruikshank from his own drawing (British Museum. Dept. of Prints and Drawings)*

carved by Henry Webber placed in Poets' Corner in Westminster Abbey on the wall opposite his grave. It unfortunately contrives to be both unbalanced and stolid, despite a design so dramatic that it 'not a little scandalized' Charles Lamb.

Garrick's fellow actors commemorated him more suitably. They founded a dining club in imitation of the various Shakespeare clubs and societies, of one of which Garrick himself had been a member. The new club was called The School of Garrick and its members met, each wearing a silver medal of Garrick, once a month during the winter season. The club survived into the next century, but Michael Kelly, the singer, who had been a member, described it as extinct by 1826.

Under the terms of Garrick's will his widow faithfully kept up his two homes, and they became slightly mouldering museums for the interested visitor until after her death in 1823, when everything was dispersed in sales. Relics of Garrick have become treasured possessions of succeeding generations of actors and theatrical historians.

Dr Johnson is reported to have offered to write his old friend's life, a proposal which for obscure reasons unfortunately came to nothing. It would be unkind to leave Oliver Goldsmith's mock epitaph in *The Retaliation,* full of truths as it is, as the last word, since it is itself an attack, provoked by Garrick's extempore couplet:

> Here lies Nolly Goldsmith, for shortness call'd Noll,
> Who wrote like an angel, but talk'd like poor Poll.

Goldsmith begins his portrait:

> Here lies David Garrick, describe me, who can,
> An abridgment of all that was pleasant in man;
> As an actor, confess'd without rival to shine:
> As a wit, if not first, in the very first line:
> Yet, with talents like these, and an excellent heart,
> The man had his failings, a dupe to his art.
> Like an ill-judging beauty, his colours he spread,
> And beplaster'd with rouge his own natural red.
> On the stage he was natural, simple, affecting;
> 'Twas only that when he was off he was acting.

MRS YATES, *in the* CHARACTER *of the* TRAGIC MUSE,

Reciting the MONODY *to the* MEMORY *of* MR GARRICK.

Published as the Act directs, by Harrison & Cº May 1,1783.

47 *Mary Ann Yates
as the Tragic Muse
reciting Sheridan's
'Verses to the
Memory of
Garrick'.
Engraving by
J. Heath after
T. Stothard 1783*

Johnson's tribute, from his *Life of Edmund Smith,* was
chosen by Mrs Garrick for the monument she placed in
Lichfield Cathedral – and perhaps we may be content with
it: 'I am disappointed by that stroke of death, which has
eclipsed the gaiety of nations and impoverished the
publick stock of harmless pleasure'.

Further Reading

WORKS BY GARRICK

The Diary of David Garrick, being a record of his memorable trip to Paris in 1751; ed. by R. C. Alexander. New York: Oxford University Press, American Branch, 1928. Reprinted New York: Arno Press. ISBN 0-450-85524-4

The Journal of David Garrick, describing his visit to France and Italy in 1763; ed. by G. W. Stone. New York: Modern Language Association of America, 1939. (Revolving Fund series, 10.) Reprinted Millwood, N.Y.: Kraus Reprint Co. ISBN 0-527-32560-0

The Letters of David Garrick; ed. by D. M. Little and G. M. Kahrl. 3 vols. London: Oxford University Press, 1963

The Plays of David Garrick; ed. by H. W. Pedicord and F. L. Bergmann. Carbondale: Southern Illinois University Press. Vols. 1-2 (of 6) announced for December 1979. ISBN 0-8093-0862-2 and 0-8093-0863-0

The Poetical Works of David Garrick, Esq. 2 vols. London: George Kearsley, 1785. Reprinted New York: Arno Press, 1968

WORKS ABOUT GARRICK

Barton, M.   *Garrick.* London: Faber and Faber, 1948.

Burnim, K. A.   *David Garrick: director.* Carbondale: Southern Illinois University Press, 1973. (Arcturus Books Paperbacks series.) ISBN 0-8093-0625-5

Deelman, C.   *The Great Shakespeare Jubilee.* London: Michael Joseph, 1964

Oman, C.   *David Garrick.* London: Hodder and Stoughton, 1958. ISBN 0-340-00556-4

Pedicord, H. W.   *The theatrical public in the time of Garrick.* Carbondale: Southern Illinois University Press, 1966. (Arcturus Books Paperbacks series.) ISBN 0-8093-0222-5

Perrin, M.   *David Garrick: homme de théâtre.* 2 vols. Lille: Atelier Reproduction des Thèses, Université de Lille III, 1978. ISBN 2-7295-0097-9

Price, C.   *Theatre in the age of Garrick.* Oxford: Basil Blackwell, 1973. ISBN 0-631-14790-X

Stein, E. P.   *David Garrick: dramatist.* New York: Modern Language Association of America, 1938. (Revolving Fund series, 7.) Reprinted New York: Arno Press. ISBN 0-405-08994-5, and Millwood, N.Y.: Kraus Reprint Co. ISBN 0-527-86100-6

Stone, G. W. & Kahrl, G. M.   *David Garrick: a critical biography.* Carbondale: Southern Illinois University Press. Announced for publication. ISBN 0-8093-0931-9

Tait, H.   'Garrick, Shakespeare, and Wilkes.' *British Museum Quarterly,* vol. XXIV, 1961, pp. 100-107

List of Exhibits

I-V

1. Brown velvet suit formerly belonging to Garrick
Museum of London 28-92
2. Portrait by Pompeo Batoni, dated 1764, of Garrick wearing the brown velvet suit in Rome. (Photograph)
Ashmolean Museum Oxford
3. Red cloth coat and white cloth waistcoat, thought to have been worn by Garrick as Macbeth
Lent anonymously
4. Engraving by R. Laurie and J. Whittle after W. Hogarth showing the proportions of Garrick and Quin, 1797
BM Dept of P. & D. Ee.3-122
5. Silhouette of Hogarth and Garrick by S. Ireland, 1799
BM Dept of P. & D Ee.3-63
6. Garrick as Richard III. Engraving by W. Hogarth and C. Grignion after W. Hogarth
BM Dept of P. & D. 1868-8-22-1569
7. Garrick as Richard III. Mezzotint by J. Dixon after N. Dance
BM Dept of P. & D. Ee.3-124
8. Garrick and Mrs Pritchard in *Macbeth*. Mezzotint by V. Green after J. Zoffany
BM Dept of P. & D. 1902-10-11-2295
9. *Copy of a letter taken from the London Daily Post . . .* [1743]. (On the dispute about actors' pay that led to the quarrel between Garrick and Charles Macklin)
BL 938.c. 6(46)
10. *The Case of Charles Macklin comedian* [1743]
BL 1855.c.4 (41)
11. *Mr Garrick's answer to Mr Macklin's case* 1743
BL 641.d.31 (4)

12. Newspaper advertisement for Garrick's first performance as Richard III at Goodman's Fields
BL 939.d.1
13. Brass token for Goodman's Fields Theatre
BM Dept of M. & L. A. Montague Guest 178
14. MS. list by Charles Burney of Garrick's parts
BL 938.d.20
15. *A clear stage and no favour,* [1742] (Comparing Garrick and Quin)
BL 11630.f.74
16. Garrick : *An essay on acting,* 1744
BL 642.d.27 (5)
17. Samuel Johnson : *Prologue and epilogue spoken at the opening of the theatre in Drury-Lane,* 1747
BL C.71.ff.5
18. Theatrical steelyards of 1750. Satirical engraving by P. O'Brien
BM Dept of P. & D. Ee.3-186
19. *Reasons why David Garrick Esq. should not appear on the stage,* 1759. (By Garrick ?)
BL 839.h.13
20. Mr and Mrs Garrick. Engraving by H. Bourne after W. Hogarth
BM Dept of P. & D. 1872-10-12-2206
21. Hampton House and the Shakespeare Temple. Coloured aquatint by J. C. Stadler after J. Farington
BM Dept of P. & D. 1948-4-10-57
22. Marble statue of Shakespeare by Louis François Roubiliac
BM Dept of M. & L. A.
23. Terracotta maquette for the Roubiliac statue
Victoria & Albert Museum
24. Painting by Adrien Carpentiers showing Roubiliac holding a Shakespeare statue maquette, 1762. (Photograph)
National Portrait Gallery 303

VI Shakespeare Jubilee, 1769

25. Garrick as Steward of the Stratford Jubilee, 1769. Mezzotint by J. Saunders after B. van der Gucht
BM Dept of P. & D. 1902-10-11-4098
26. Handbill listing the events of the Jubilee
BL C.61.e.2
27. Garrick and a bust of Shakespeare. Mezzotint by V. Green after T. Gainsborough
BM Dept of P. & D. 1870-6-25-629
28. MS. letter from F. Wheler to Garrick, dated 1767 which gave rise to the Jubilee
BL C.61.e.2
29, 30. Mulberry wood casket by Thomas Davies containing the document conferring on Garrick the freedom of the borough of Stratford-upon-Avon
BM Dept of M. & L. A. 64, 8-16, 1 & 2
31. Shakespeare Jubilee silver medal : obverse, and wooden case
BM Dept of M. & L. A. 64, 8-16, 5
reverse
BM Dept of C. & M. M4766
32. Garrick : *Ode upon dedicating a building and erecting a statue to Shakespeare,* 1769, with MS. corrections
BL 1346.k.43
33. Garrick delivering the Jubilee Ode. Engraving from *Town and Country Magazine,* 1769
BL L.R.271.c.8
34. Engraved title page of *Shakespeare's Garland,* 1769 (Songs by Garrick)
BL C.61.e.2
35. *Garrick's vagary, or England run mad,* 1769
BL 161.e.30

VII Shakespearian Tragedy

36. Garrick as King Lear. Mezzotint by J. McArdell after B. Wilson
BM Dept of P. & D. Ee.3-111
37. Sketches by W. H. Brooke of the four sides of the mulberry wood casket (no.29) : the design for the back based on no.36 *BL C.61.e.2*
38. Garrick as Hamlet. Mezzotint by J. McArdell after B. Wilson
BM Dept of P. & D. Ee.3-106
39. G. C. Lichtenberg's account of Garrick as Hamlet. In *Deutsches Museum*, vol. 1, 1776
BL P.P.4748. aa.
40. Henry Fielding's description of Garrick as Hamlet. In *Tom Jones*, vol. 6, 1749 *BL C.71. cc.7*
41. Joshua Steele's transcription of an actor's delivery of 'To be or not to be'
In *Prosodia rationalis*, 1779
BL 73.g.16
42. John Hill : *To David Garrick Esq; the petition of I*, 1759. (On Garrick's pronunciation)
BL 11798.aa.15
43. Nahum Tate : *The history of King Lear*, 1699. Garrick's copy
BL 644.i.47
44. Shakespeare : *King Lear*. Second quarto, [1619]. Garrick's copy
BL C.34.k.19
45. Shakespeare : *King Lear*, 1756, used as promptbook at Drury Lane Theatre *BL C.119.dd.22*
46. Shakespeare : *King Lear ... altered ... by D. Garrick*, 1786
BL 11763.ppp.78

VIII-IX Garrick the Actor

47. Sword and scabbard, thought to have belonged to Garrick
Lent anonymously
48. Wig of brown natural hair, thought to have been worn by Garrick as Abel Drugger in Jonson's *The alchemist* *Lent anonymously*
49. Garrick as Abel Drugger with Burton and Palmer in *The alchemist*. Mezzotint by J. Dixon after J. Zoffany *BM Dept of P. & D.*
1902-10-11-745
50. Garrick as Abel Drugger. Drawing by J. Roberts
BM Dept of P. & D. LB 65
51. Engraving after Louisa Lane showing Garrick wigless. (Likeness endorsed by the actor Jack Bannister) *Lent anonymously*
52. Garrick, with wig, as Bayes in Buckingham's *The rehearsal*. Drawing by J. Roberts
BM Dept of P. & D. LB 69

53. Garrick as Bayes, wigless. Anonymous ink drawing
BM Dept of P. & D. Ee.3-177
54. Silver plated ladle, with Garrick's crest on the back
Lent anonymously
55. Garrick, Parsons and others in Vanbrugh's *The provok'd wife*. Mezzotint by J. Finlayson after J. Zoffany
BM Dept of P. & D. Ee.3-175
56. Garrick as Sir John Brute in *The provok'd wife*. Drawing by J. Roberts
BM Dept of P. & D. LB 68
57. A scene from Garrick's *Miss in her teens*, 1747. Two engravings
BM Dept of P. & D.
1868-8-8-3823
58. Garrick : *Miss in her teens*, 1747
BL Ashley 3247
59. Garrick as Demetrius in E. Young's *The Brothers*. Drawing by J. Roberts
BM Dept of P. & D. LB 66
60. Fanny Burney's description of Garrick as Ranger in B. Hoadley's *The suspicious husband*. In *Evelina*, vol. 1, 1779
BL 12650.a.128
61. Garrick : *The farmer's return*, 1762, with engraved frontispiece after W. Hogarth *BL 163.m.3*
62. Sir Joshua Reynolds : *Johnson on Garrick*, 1816
BL C.134.b.7(1) & G.16313
63. Garrick : *The theatrical candidates*, 1775 *BL 83.a.21(1)*
64. Garrick as Romeo and Mrs Bellamy as Juliet. Engraving by R. S. Ravenet after B. Wilson
BM Dept of P. & D. Ee.3-183
65. Playbill advertising a performance with Garrick as Romeo, 1755
BL 10825.f.19
66. Shakespeare : *Romeo and Juliet* (altered by Garrick), 1778, with engraved frontispiece after B. Wilson (no.64) *BL 11765.aa.32*
67. Garrick as Kitely in Jonson's *Every man in his humour*. Mezzotint by J. Finlayson after Sir J. Reynolds
BM Dept of P. & D.
1902-10-11-2086
68. Jonson : *Every man in his humour* (altered by Garrick). Bell's British Theatre, vol. 2, 1776 *BL 82.d.6*
69. Aaron Hill : *Zara* (altered by Garrick). Bell's British Theatre, vol. 1, 1776, with engraved plate after J. Roberts *BL 82.d.5*
70. Garrick : *A Christmas tale*, 1774, with etched frontispiece by P J. de Loutherbourg *BL 1509/769*
71. Garrick : *Lilliput* (music by D. Corri), 1817 *BL Music G.243*
72. Shakespeare : *A midsummer night's dream*. First quarto, 1600. Garrick's copy *BL C.34.k.29*

73. Shakespeare : *A midsummer night's dream*, 1734
BL 11763.ppp.69
74. MS. additions by Garrick to *A midsummer night's dream*, 1763
BL Add. MS. 39,302 f.57 & f.59
75. Shakespeare : *A midsummer night's dream* (altered by Garrick and George Colman), 1763
BL 163.i.3
76. Garrick : *To Mr Gray on his Odes*, [1757] *BL G.984 (16)*
77. Garrick : *Heart of Oak* (music by William Boyce). In *Clio and Euterpe*, vol. 3, [1762] *BL Music D.412a*
78. George Colman and Garrick : *The clandestine marriage*, 1766
BL 841.e.71
79. Garrick : *Occasional prologue ... 10 June 1776*. In *Poetical Works*, vol. 2, 1785 *BL 238.d.38*
80. Garrick : *The meeting of the company*, 1926 *BL X.900/2058*

XI-XII Lethe, etc.

81. Linen and cotton wall hanging, plate-printed in blue with a design illustrating Garrick's *Lethe*. (Photograph enlarged)
Victoria & Albert Museum T.75-1914
82, 83. Kitty Clive as Mrs. Riot. Two Bow porcelain figures, glazed and in the biscuit state ; design based on engraving by C. Mosley (no.87) *BM Dept of M .& L. A. Porcelain cat.l 6 & 7*
84. Henry Woodward as the 'modern fine gentleman'. Bow porcelain figure ; design based on mezzotint after F. Hayman (no.89)
BM Dept of M .& L. A. Porcelain cat.l.5
85. Wedgwood jasper portrait medallion of Garrick, 1777
BM Dept of M. & L. A. Pottery cat.l.81
86. Garrick as Lord Chalkstone in *Lethe*. Anonymous engraving
BM Dept of P. & D. Ee.3-128
87. Kitty Clive as Mrs. Riot. Engraving by C. Mosley (Photograph) *BM Dept of P. & D. Burnley Theatrical portraits vol.II. f.102*
88. Henry Woodward as the 'modern fine gentleman'. Drawing by Francis Hayman
Fitzwilliam Museum Cambridge
89. Henry Woodward as the 'modern fine gentleman'. Mezzotint by J. McArdell after F. Hayman
BM Dept of M. & L. A.
90. J. L. Fäsch : Six drawings of actors and actresses
BM Dept of P. & D.
1931-5-9-250 . . . 255

91. Twenty Liverpool tiles, black or sepia designs depicting actors and actresses, after J. L. Fäsch
BN Dept of M. & L. A.
Pottery cat.E.166

XIII Garrick as Manager of Drury Lane Theatre

92. Interior of Drury Lane Theatre, decorated by R. Adam. Engraving by B. Pastorini
BM Dept of P. & D.
1880-9-11-1022
93. Engraving showing Bridges Street façade, Drury Lane Theatre. (Photograph, enlarged)
BL 11826.r. vol.XI
94. A scene from Sheridan's *The school for scandal.* Engraving, 1778. (Photograph, enlarged)
BL 1871.b.12(2)
95. *An Act* for securing the Theatrical Fund, 1776
BL 011795.ee.9
96. Contract between Garrick, etc. and Charles Macklin, 1759
BL Add.MS. 27,925
97. Accounts of expenditure of Drury Lane Theatre, 1774-5
BL Add.MS.44,919
98. Bronze token by L. Pingo, 1772
BM Dept of M. & L. A.
Montague Guest 1464
99. Bronze token by J. Kirk, 1772
BM Dept of C. & M. M4769
100. Bronze token by J. Kirk, 1776
BM Dept of C. & M. M4811★
101. MS. notebook kept by W. Hopkins the prompter
BL 11826.r. vol.VIII
102. J. G. Noverre : Lettres sur les arts imitateurs, vol.2, 1817
BL 7907.bbb.2
103. Garrick : *The Fribbleriad,* 1761
BL 644.k.18(2)
104. *An historical and succinct account of the late riots at the Theatres,* 1763 *BL 1347.e.26*
105. F. Gentleman : *The theatres,* 1772 *BL 11630.d. 3(14)*
106. W. Kenrick : *A letter to David Garrick Esq.* (*Love in the suds*), 1772 *BL 644.l.21*
107. Garrick : *The sick monkey,* 1765 *BL Ashley 3249*
108. W. Combe : *Sanitas daughter of Aesculapius,* 1772
BL 11630.f.20

XIV Garrick's Death

109. Garrick led off the stage by Time. Mezzotint by R. Laurie after T. Parkinson, 1779
BM Dept of P. & D.
1902-10-11-3027
110. Invitation to Garrick's funeral, engraved by W. Darling
BM Dept of P. & D. Ee.3-224
111. *The life and death of David Garrick,* 1779 (An account of his funeral) *BL G.14432*
112. Mourning ring for Garrick
Mrs Michael Wynne
113. Wedgwood black basalt intaglio bust of Garrick
BM Dept of M. & L. A.
Pottery cat.l.519
114. Sheridan : *Verses to the memory of Garrick,* 1779 with frontispiece by P. J. de Loutherbourg
BL Ashley 5044
115. L. McNally : *The apotheosis of Punch,* 1779 *BL 163.h.10*
116. Silver medal of Garrick by L. Pingo, probably worn for meetings of 'The School of Garrick'
BM Dept of C. & M.
1866-7-14-61
117. Engraved invitation to a meeting of 'The School of Garrick'
BL L.R.23.c.5(12)
118. Mrs. Garrick, 1820. Etching by R. Cruikshank
BM Dept of P. & D
1865-11-11-2585
119. Admission ticket to Garrick's houses, with a wafer medallion portrait
BM Dept of M. & L. A. 64,8-16,7
120. O. Goldsmith : *The retaliation* 1774 *BL Ashley 3271*
121. S. Johnson's epitaph on Garrick in his *Life of Smith,* 1779
BL 1162.e.9 (vol. 4)

XV-XVII The Garrick Plays

122. Garrick's will. (With a photograph of the page detailing his bequest to the British Museum)
Public Record Office PROB. 1/16
123. Sale catalogue of Garrick's library, 1823 *BL 825.kk.24(1)*
124. Edward Capell's MS. catalogue of the Garrick plays *BL 643.l.30*
125. J. Shirley : *The gentleman of Venice,* 1655. (BM binding by Tuckett on a Garrick play : crimson straight-grained morocco leather tooled in gold) *BL C.34.e.4*

126. Binding tool of Garrick's arms used by BM bindery, (with an enlarged photograph of its impression). *H.M.S.O. Bindery*
127. J. Brownsmith : *The theatrical alphabet* 1767, Garrick's copy, tooled with his name
BL C.134.b.12
128. *Hycke Scorner,* [1515 ?]
BL C.21.c.4
129. J. Rastell : *The nature of the four elements,* [1520 ?]
BL C.39.b.17
130. *Everyman,* [1526 ?]
BL C.21.c.17
131. John Heywood : *The four P's,* 1544 *BL C.34.c.43*
132. *A mery geste of Robyn Hoode,* [1560 ?] *BL C.21.c.63*
133. Thomas Kyd : *The Spanish tragedy,* 1592 *BL C.34.d.7*
134. Shakespeare : *Othello,* 1622, wrongly imposed in Sig. C
BL C.34.k.33
135. Shakespeare : *Henry IV,* Part I, 1598. (With photograph of letter bound in it) *BL C.34.k.5★*
136. Shakespeare : *Love's labour's lost,* 1631. (Copy formerly belonging to King Charles I) *BL C.34.k.21*
137. Ben Jonson : *The characters of two royall masques,* [1608], with his MS. dedication to Queen Anne
BL C.34.d.4(1)
138. *Tom Tyler and his wife,* 1661, with Richard Smith's MS. note at the end *BL 643.d.63*
139. *The Knight of the Swanne,* [1565 ?] *BL C.21 c 67*
140. W. Mountfort : *Greenwich Park* 1691. (From the Harleian Library) *BL 644.h.68*
141. C. Tourneur : *The revenger's tragedy,* 1607. (Copy used by Robert Dodsley for *A select collection of old plays,* 1744)
BL C.34.e.11
142. *The works of Ben Jonson,* ed. Peter Whalley, vol. 1, 1756
BL 673.f.13
143. T. Percy : *Reliques of ancient English poetry,* vol.1, 1765
BL 11626.bbb.36
144. Reader's application signed by Charles Lamb for 'Garrick plays from l5'
BL Dept of P.B. Archives 5c
145. C. Lamb : *Specimens of the English dramatic poets,* 1835.
BL 11771.bb.1